SONATA
IN THE KEY OF BEING

POEMS
BY

SUSAN SPAETH CHERRY

 CHICAGO SPECTRUM PRESS
LOUISVILLE, KENTUCKY 40207

CHICAGO SPECTRUM PRESS
4824 BROWNSBORO CENTER
LOUISVILLE, KENTUCKY 40207
502-899-1919

Printed in the U.S.A.

10 9 8 7 6 5 4 3 2 1

ISBN: 1-58374-020-1

For my daughters, Alison and Erica,
who have given birth to the poet in me

CONTENTS

ALLEGRO NON TRÓPPO

LARGO

VIVACE

ALLEGRO
NON
TRÓPPO

THE IRONY OF BEING HUMAN

The quest for individualness
begins with "No!" in diaper days
and keeps on blinking all our lives
like strings of colored Christmas lights.
It sings in the pink, spiked hair
of the child just turned thirteen,
in the twenty-something's
nipple pierce, in the midlifer's
tussle with therapy, in the senior's
struggle to master the sax.

Yet as we strive to be distinct,
we seek to lose the very selves
we chisel so compulsively,
merging with another's flesh
till oneness summons blissfulness,
meditating till our brainbirth
dissipates like morning fog,
chanting to a higher power
with scores of other thirsting tongues—
never quite able to reconcile

the need to be Me
with the need to be We.

STRADDLING TWO WORLDS

Opaline flakes
flutter into twilight
like a flight of frozen butterflies,
alighting on December's bones.
Abandoning the magazine
that tells her how to be a teen,
the seventh grader grabs the boots
she'd never dare to wear to school
and charges out the kitchen door,
enchanted as a puppy
who has just discovered mud.

She scoops and tongues
the untouched white,
monograms a neighbor's lawn,
makes an angel facing God,
then capers down the silent street,
laughing as she loses her balance
on pavement slippery as her age.

Her hands and nose begin to numb;
she heads for home where messages wait
from friends who've called to chat about
the newest couple in her class
and the latest hue of nail paint.

HAIKU MUSINGS ON HUMAN NATURE

I

On Seeking a Spouse

Decorated cakes
often look much tastier
than they really are.

II

On Falling in Love

The mountain dazzles,
then disappears in the fog
when we least expect.

III

On Married Life

Whine of complaining
is served more frequently than
wine of dialogue.

IV

On Pretending Things Will Change

The sandal that rubs
continues to irritate
till you take it off.

V

On Losing a Spouse

Men and women are
kites, stranded in the naked
branches of their past.

NEW ORLEANS GUMBO

I

Bourbon Street tourists
toss out
their proscriptions and inhibitions
like Mardi Gras beads.

Far
from their children and bosses and bills,
they change
into satyrs and Sirens and satans,

imbibing in potions
that give them the power
to see only now
and forget about later.

At dawn they'll lament
that their heads are aflame
and their stomachs, afloat
as they crawl into bed

to escape from Escape,
the sweet and tyrannical
lovechild
of Stress and Human Nature.

II

The St. Charles trolley clatters past
the mansions of the Garden District,
out of place as cymbals in a lullaby.

Beaming at Corinthian columns
and wrought-iron railings
coifed and painted like Southern belles,

it hails the limos and Mercedes
lounging under balconies
adorned in leaded glass and lace,

while riders on their way to work
open their windows to breathe the green
aroma of inheritance.

III

A horse-drawn hearse escorted
by a shove of rags and business suits
rattles to the graveyard
while a jocund jazz band
plays "The Saints Come Marchin' In."

The arms of Quarter locals
load the casket on a concrete shelf
to keep the swamp from gobbling

the body of the Chicken Man,
adored eccentric of the street,

while at the voodoo temple
just across the way, mourners
place their cigarettes
and flasks at shrines remembering
the uncrowned king of New Orleans.

SHOPPING FOR THE BIG DAY

Cascading
from the hanger
like a waterfall,
the gown dazzles
my daughter's endless
sense of possibility.

She sweeps its skirt
across her cheek,
runs her fingers
over its beads,
fishes it from
the river of ruffles
overflowing
into the aisle,

and flounces
into the fitting room,
emerging
moments later
with the dazzle
of a sequin
in a box
of humble buttons,

15

while I turn weepy
as April, who
gives birth to buds
it savors
for a week or two,
then loses to May's
alluring embrace.

THE MERCURY PLUMMETS IN MINUTES

The sun lingers in autumn's kitchen,
sipping one last cup of tea,

while winter tantrums on the porch,
furious that its favorite chair

is taken by a loiterer
arrayed from head to toe in gold.

Sawing through the deadbolt lock,
the interloper barges in

and knocks the kettle off the stove,
thumbs its nose at guest and host,

and dances on the tabletop,
ripping the cloth of coziness,

jovial as a Roman king
about to start a six-month feast.

FOR MY JEWISH DAUGHTERS

December arrives bedecked in bulbs
of every hue, pine and velvet around her neck,
a gaudy tiara of expectation
pinned into her frosted hair.

Awestruck by her dazzling mien,
you beg to have a baubled tree,
to sit on Santa's padded lap,
to carol dressed in green and red.

Your longing tramples on my heart
like reindeer feet, demanding to know
why I've chosen to deprive you
of the season's treats.

Perhaps some day you'll understand
I'm giving you Identity,
which hasn't the shimmer of tinsel and ribbon,
but lights a lifetime steadily.

TEENAGE MOM

Towing her fleet
through the rush hour billows,
she anchors in a cove of briefcases,
cracking her gum,
fiddling with her plastic beads,
slapping her kids
as they bob like buoys in their seats.

Gradually, her eyelids droop
like branches full of unpicked fruit,
till she doesn't notice her toddler pinball
through the throng of pinstriped knees
or hear the scream
as her preschooler misses
the hanging ring he jumped to reach,
or feel her baby
inch toward the denim cliff
of her knees.

The wheels stop; her eldest
shakes her by the sleeve,
and half-asleep, she scuttles her brood
through the disapproval
that chokes the car like a cheap cigar,
quickly vanishing from view
but not from the stare of memory.

HEALTH

knocks on our door
before we are born
and moves in
with a suitcase
it never unpacks,
a humble houseguest
who takes out the garbage
and readies the beds
for restorative sleep,

numb to ungratefulness,
eager to please
until it decides
to take a vacation,
leaving us frantic
to hear the hourly
whoosh of its broom,
to view its baskets
of folded clothes,
to inhale the aromas
it sends from the stove.

We stuff it with hugs
upon its return,
fetch its slippers

and paper and pipe
for a day or two—
then hand it a rag,
relegating it
back to the realm
of the ignored.

YELLOWSTONE

You watch the water
leap from the arms of Mother River
into the swirl below the escarpment,
where splendor floats on diamond rafts.

You ride your shutter button
like a photographic pogo stick,
hardly noticing sunburned tourists
who toss superlatives over the rail,
then scramble to the shops nearby,
where souvenir shirts and key chains wait.

Glued to the mist as the minutes blow past,
you listen intently to waterfall whispers
the rest of the world cannot perceive—
including me, who could never accept
that although the same current churns in our veins,
we're different as stones at the cascade's toe.

But as I watch your wild joy
form rainbows in the milky spray,
I envy all that makes you You,
the person I hope to know with time.

AUTOPSY

When they sawed into
the maestro's skull
to find
why he
collapsed
and died
on the
podium,
Italian
phrases
in fuchsia
and taupe,
sharps
and flats,
fermatas,
slurs, and
millions
of notes
with dots
and flags
surged out
like drops of a
waterfall, drowning
the room in sparkles of
sound, and the coroner
confidently pronounced
the cause of death
as overdose.

TO LAST YEAR'S POEM

You started as a gawky kid,
the kind who wears "kick me" signs
taped to his back, the butt
of every playground prank.

I fed you tidbits from the Muse
to build your strength,
cursing as rolls of fat took shape
in all the wrong places.

I made you do
push-ups and pull-ups and sit-ups,
refusing to ever allow you to rest
until you became

a David of words,
and I fell in love
with your muscular nouns
and sinewy verbs,

unaware that next year,
you'd transform
from the he-man I madly adored
into an oaf I'd forever abhor.

CONFERENCE

We sit at a table and chat
about spelling, science, and math,
slipping attraction under the stack
of exams you'll grade this afternoon.

Our wedding rings gleam
in the green classroom light,
illuminating our every word
like burnished police,

keeping impropriety
from picking the locks
we installed on our doors
years before we'd ever met.

Another father lurks in the hall;
I shake your hand a little too long
and head for my car,
damning the rules

for damming the waters
of what could be, waters teeming
with living creatures whose neon hues
mute in the sea-dark of moral comport.

INVISIBILITY

Fifteen teens,

chomping gossip like popcorn
on my living room floor,

ruminating about the dates
they had last week,

singing random bars of tunes
that drizzle on the plunk of shoes
they've planted by the door.

I rattle through the home
where I was mistress just an hour ago,
a laundry-toting motherghost,

exposed and yet invisible,

reveling as gab and hormones
toast each other jovially,
marveling at how glorious it is

to be and not to be

until the curse of curfew
turns me back to muscle, flesh, and bone,

just in time to clear the cups
where jokes and flirtations
have settled like dust.

THE RATIONALIST'S HANDICAP

The cellist
celebrates
the marriage
of sound and soul,
sliding her bow
across the strings
with the holiness
of the Creator.
I weep
as she whirls
into worlds
I covet
but cannot know,
simply because
I was born
from the bloodless
womb of thought,
where the seed
of divinity
cannot grow.

Allegro non Tróppo

THE SHARPENER'S LAMENT

The streets weren't paved with silence
in the old country, where women like you
spewed from their homes at the sound of my bell,
babies on their aproned hips,
bladed bouquets in their outstretched hands.

They'd lean on my pushcart
and feed each other the latest tales
as I pressed their knives
against my wheel's stubbled cheek.

Here, the women dress in suits
and get their news from commentators.
They have no use for kitchen knives,
which can't sell stock or write a brief
or microwave a frozen pizza.

My son says I should give my cart
to the history museum down the road
and get myself a "real job,"
like selling computers or T.V.s.

But there's something about this wheel of mine
that keeps me going
when life is spinning
until it's too dizzy to walk a straight line.

29

Ah, yes, your knives.
Four dollars, please.
Look for me again next week.

Allegro non Tróppo

COCKTAIL PARTY

You approach with a smile
wide as an octave of piano keys.

I beam in turn, wondering whether you can see
the spinach dip between my teeth,

pondering how to shake your hand
and hold my glass and beaded bag.

"So nice to see you again," you croon.

I excavate my catacombs
for clues of where we've met before,

finding only hollow bones
I magically transform to words.

We talk about our work as if
we each knew what the other did.

I ask about your family, avoiding
terms like "spouse" and "kids."

Then suddenly, our mouths are dry.

We sip our wine, entangled
in the sticky web of etiquette.

You eye the table of hors d'oeuvres,
say you need another drink,

and with a "Hope to see you soon,"
slink across the crowded room

to re-enact our scene.

THE UNKNOWN

plunks itself on my welcome mat
and whines to get into my cozy home.

Parting the curtains, I peer at it
with mistrustfulness, unsure if it

will rub itself against my legs
or ravage my defenselessness.

I hammer a spoon against a pan
to shoo it away, while my children,

who know nothing of fleas or claws or teeth,
plead for me to keep the creature.

Fighting the urge to bolt the door,
I lay a bowl of scraps on the steps

and hope that a purr
will gobble my fear.

SEVENTEEN

My universe expands with pride
when I see you parade in tank top and shorts,
exploding the gaze like a supernova.

My eyes hike through your valleys and hills,
amazed at what Nature's fingers have shaped
from baby fat and lanky bone.

I pray that the years will continue to beam
on your beauty like a harvest moon,
obscuring the partial eclipse of my joy

by the fiery orb of covetousness,
which reels through the void of middle age,
defying the pull of maternal love.

Allegro non Tróppo

WE WALK

by the lake after evening retires,
summer licking our sunburned limbs
with her sticky tongue.

Fireflies spatter the skin of night
like neon freckles, hailing mates
with silent streaks of yellow-green,

fusing on sodden pillows of heat,
then breaking apart again
into the dark.

So it has been for fifteen years
of nighttime strolls when you and I,
attracted by each other's light,

have mated with our winged minds,
dappling blackness with flecks of gold
before we fly off to our separate homes.

A DORM GOES CONDO

Peregrine machine
seizes its prey,
hungry for havoc.

Doorways cave in
like lips on a mouth
with its dentures out;

layers of wallpaper
peel in ringlets
ribboned in dust;

rock stars writhe
on splintered glass,
decapitated in their frames.

Carefully crafted,
brick by brick,
the student sanctum

weathers decades
of Nature's tricks,
yet crumbles in minutes

in Greed's rugged grip.

ON VIEWING
"THE TREASURES OF TUTANKHAMEN"

I stand in line two hours to see
antiquity encased in glass—
a chiseled, alabaster boat;
a death mask cast in solid gold;
a necklace for the sun god Ra;
a dagger with a jeweled haft.

I summon chariots of awe
to carry me to ecstasy
befitting wonders crafted
thirty centuries ago.
The wheels spin, but can't advance
across modernity's terrain,
paved with imitation
of the very slickest grade.

I leave through the museum store,
where scores are clamoring to buy
mummies, statues, rings, and shields
that no one will be able
to distinguish from the real thing.

IRONY

This mass of plastic and circuitry
has cut the cord that once connected
my world to the womb of limitation.

I take it for granted like daylight or air,
forgetting that not so long ago,
I calculated my taxes by hand,

strained my back from hauling
stacks of *Readers' Guides,* waited a week
for my mail to mosey across the ocean.

How strange to know who conceived
the reaper, the steamboat, and the cotton gin—
none of which I've ever seen—

but to be unable to answer the question
my daughter asked at lunch today:
"Who invented the computer?"

ODE TO A BREAST

You enter the world sewn like a snap
on the satin of infancy,

sleeping for years on a futon of bone
until puberty's fingers shake you awake

and feed you ambrosia to fatten you up.
You rise like a loaf that is soon to become

a temptation no male can ever resist.
You bathe in the melted butter of touch

until suddenly, motherhood floods you in white,
and you hanker for kisses from miniature lips,

weeping whenever you hear the cry
of a babe you don't know on the bus or the train.

When you hang out to dry on the backyard line,
you flag the attention of passersby,

who prefer to focus on lilies and roses.
And soon, it comes time for the annual rite

of squeezing into a glass bikini
and posing on film for the critical eye,

wondering if even the tiniest speck
has blemished your flesh,

sentencing you to forever forget
the bliss you once gave, the life you sustained.

BREAKING THE RULES

I'm picking apples
on this, the holiest
day of the year,
the day I'm supposed
to atone for my sins
in the straight-lipped
ritual of synagogue.

The sweetness
of the hanging fruit
cannot assuage
the guilt that nibbles
at my core,
a guilt the hands
of tradition planted,
seed by seed.

Capped and shawled
in branch and leaf,
I bless the earth's
fecundity and wonder
if God will punish me
for hallowing
this arc-less, scroll-less
sanctuary of red and green,

where I can ponder
all I said and did last year
far better than the place
that I'm supposed to be.

ELEVENTH BIRTHDAY

June turns to January
overnight.

Smiles stand
on their golden heads.

Cheeks redden
regularly as stoplights.

The telephone cord
becomes a lifeline;

a mother's arms,
a deathtrap.

A silver word
can burnish a day.

An eyebrow raised
can tarnish a week.

"Fatal" means an errant hair
or broken nail.

"Futile" means unable
to be solved in seconds.

Eleventh birthday.

Twelve waits panting
across the sea.

43

CONTEMPLATING TIME

Once the summer
dangled down the back of the year
like a heavy braid,

unmoving in the restlessness
that blew through my life
from June to September.

I'd sit behind a makeshift stand,
selling cups of lemonade,
wishing the pennies

customers dropped on my plastic plate
could buy a quick passage
to second grade.

I'd lie in bed as the evening blued
and listen to the sonic booms
that split the summer heat in two,

marveling as the grown-ups
on the screened-in porch below my room
complained about the way time zooms,

unaware that all too soon,
summer would become a lily
lasting but a single day.

OBLIGATION

pock-marks life
like a hailstone,
pitting duty against desire.

You put aside your magazine
to listen to your sister gripe
about the sap who stood her up;

you buy a birthday present
for the outgrown friend
who still insists on swapping gifts;

you ask the aunts to Christmas brunch
and hang your wish to be alone
behind the trinkets on your tree;

you greet your best friend's husband
(who you cannot stand)
with hearty kisses on the cheek;

and all the while, you smile
while the tartar of resentment builds
invisibly upon your teeth.

THE LAST DANCE RECITAL

In a theater familiar
as a grandma's kiss,

the lights go down,
and on the stage appears

my child, once too shy to even smile
at anyone she hadn't met a dozen times,

now beaming into strangers' stares,
sashaying with assuredness

that Time delivered, year by year,
in packages the size of dimes.

I wipe my eyes,
knowing that in not too long,

she'll twirl into another life,
not caring if I'm there to clap or videotape,

unaware of how I ache
to put the decades in rewind.

SIMULTANEITY

On the last warm day of the century,
I shoved my rushedness under the leaves
that shoed November's unsteady feet
and strolled like a tourist,
bedazzled by streets I'd seen hundreds of times,
hanging my eyes on branch after branch
of orange and yellow, red and green.
Jack-o-lanterns lobotomized
by tablespoons and serrated knives
grinned foolishly into the afternoon mildness,
unknowing that soon, they'd be squirrel food.

I stopped on a bridge to watch a kayak
part the hair of the water below
and suddenly noticed a curious
mass of silver and black,
floating face-down in a scatter of foliage:
a baby raccoon, bloated and limp,
as if it had swallowed
the poisons mixed into this savory day—

an exploding plane that transformed the ocean
into a salty buffet of bones; a hurricane
with insatiable cravings for everything stable;
a gunman whose table
was set with the shatterproof china of hate.

47

I gazed at the rings on the dead creature's tail,
amazed how the world's concurrently circled
with splendor and pain, and wondered
if ever I'd learn to accept
this aspect of life that no human can change.

TO MY NEIGHBOR'S BEECH

Middle age
came late this year,
waiting till after Halloween
to bald the trees
and sag the flesh
of flowers and weeds.

I stroll the street,
feeling at one
with shrubbery
no longer green
but not yet dead,
when suddenly,
I notice you,

rising like a phoenix
from an umber pyre
of crumbling leaves,
your spindly wings
ablaze with buds
that normally
appear in spring.

Astounded
at your quiet power
to make new life

while those around you
languish
in the waning light,
I wonder
what I need to do
to be like you.

THE WHY OF CRASHES

Exercising,
Poseidon stretches
magnetic arms
out of the Atlantic waves,
attracting planes
to his salty gym,
adding souls
to his workout routine
like extra weights,

while mothers and fathers,
daughters and sons,
dress in locker rooms
of angst,
the sweat of hopefulness
showered away.

OFF TO CAMP

Your smile is frayed as your cut-offs
as we carry in the duffel bags
delivered last night from cardboard wombs.

Your blue eyes flit from child to child
like butterflies seeking the sweetest nectar,
alighting on a baseball cap,
a ponytail, a silver cross.

A sweat of questions spatters your brow:
Will I be able to find my way
from the stables to the dining hall?
To sail a Sunfish by myself?
To meet someone who doesn't need
to wear a bra or shave her legs?

A counselor wearing her voice
on a braid around her neck
presents you to a jabber of girls
who'll teach you about the power of lies
as they barter for gossip at midnight's bazaar.

You clutch me as you always do
each time a first swoops into your nest
and carries you skyward, into sunshine
you can't yet see.

I stuff your pockets with reassurance
and say good-bye, barely able
to wait until I'm on the road
to drink from my own canteen of tears.

POETIC JUSTICE

Robed and gaveled
in rhythm and rhyme,

the poet summons
the unsuspecting to the stand,

exposing their deeds
like sandaled feet,

never bothering
to ask how they plead,

pretending not to care
what they think

when they're sentenced to life
in a lockup of ink.

THE HARBOR DWELLERS

They sleep beneath a quilt of mist:

fishing schooners painted red,
their sails wound like spools of thread;

upended rowboats, nosing the sky
like captive dolphins at feeding time;

motorboats stenciled in proud, black script
proclaiming names like Torch and Crypt;

reveler yachts that clink their masts
in one last toast against night's glass.

In an hour or two, they'll tango
on the polished dance floor of the lake,

but now, they wait in dawn's embrace,
each a smile on summer's face.

NUANCE

The awaited letter
signed "sincerely"
instead of "love"...

the pianist's pause
between phrases
of a Chopin prelude...

the glaze in the eyes
of the ever-smiling
dinner guest...

the quick glance back
of the child boarding
the bus for camp...

the pinch of salt
that turns the broth
into a brine...

the tint in the paint
transforming the portrait
from good to great...

Nuance
makes all the difference,
catapulting existence

from earth
to the realms
of flames and angels.

LARGO

LIFE-ACHES

brandish blades of bafflement
at the mind and ravage
the heart's unguarded empire,

planting mines that detonate
when we're asleep, digging trenches
where they await our certain arrival.

We sabotage them with complaint,
plunder them with rationalization,
impale them on our hopes and dreams,

but like the worm that remakes itself,
life-aches just regenerate, inching
into happiness in disconnected segments.

THE POWER OF NOW

I bleed like a beet
when I see the photos
in the *Times*
of jellied eyes
that quiver with questions,
of hands that carry
the past in sacks,
of feet that trudge
through unwantedness
without a map.

But then, my mini-van
dies on the street,
the computer erases
my latest poem,
the spot won't come out
of my favorite jeans,

and suddenly,
compassion flees
like a refugee
pursued by the troops
of my own
mundane reality—
soldiers trained
to loot and waste
the tenderest chambers
of the heart.

LATE!

Motherangst hovers
like a vulture,
waiting to feast
on my sanity's flesh.

Trying to read, I listen
for the click of your key
but hear only the clunk
of worry's feet.

I plead with the phone
to quell my disquiet,
but it sleeps at my side
like an apathetic cat.

I picture you lying
unlimbed on the highway,
or sobbing, half-clothed,
behind some dumpster.

The open window
catches your laugh,
and relief blows in
like an ocean breeze,

cooling the burning
sand of my night
until it transforms
into solid ice

that will bury
my capacious love
in a massive glacier
of reprimand.

BORN TOO SOON

The messages dripped on her adolescence
like Chinese water torture:

He won't respect you.

Nice girls don't.

What's yours is yours.

She learned to say No,
to muffle the static between her legs
with the pulsating music of busyness.

Then,

chanting women torched their bras,

flower children planted seeds
in the Woodstock mud,

the Beatles crooned,
"Why don't we do it in the road?"

and Chastity handed Desire the crown
he had proudly worn for generations,

becoming a hermit who wouldn't dare
to show his face at the gates of youth.

But having learned her lessons well,

she couldn't bow to the newest king,
though the world lay prostrate at his feet,
commanding her to follow its lead.

Now she lies in her husband's heat,
still caught between the stop and go
of yesterday, wondering
if the strangled love they're trying to make
would breathe with ease
if only she had come of age
a decade later.

ONE WEEK AFTER SAYING GOOD-BYE

Melancholy hovers like humidity,
sticky, thick, invisible, yet felt in every cell.

It circumscribes my every day
like haziness around the moon

and lazes on my nighttimes
like a cat who waits to suck my breath.

I box it in activity,
mail it without a return address,

but it just comes back,
a boomerang of gloominess

that will land at my feet repeatedly
until we once again embrace.

PERPETUAL QUESTION

My children sit
in the nest I built
from twigs of convention,
gobbling truths
I drop into
their open beaks:

Hard work pays off.

People treat you as you treat them.

Healthful living yields long life.

Watching their bellies
swell with the fodder
of optimism,
I wonder
if I'm fueling them
so they can fly
or fattening them up
for Reality
to seize and devour.

CONFESSION TO MY DAUGHTER

The boundary line
where you leave off
and I begin
is indistinct
as the moment one goes
from being well
to being ill.

Your life
becomes my own
when sleep
paints scenes of youth
beneath my lids,
and once again, I'm
late for class,
incompetent
behind the wheel,
despondent over
a fight with a friend.

Awake, I taste
the nuance
of your feelings
like a gourmet chef,
savoring every
forkful of smile,

washing down scowls
with the wine
of condolence.

A mother shouldn't
be her child,

but love has a way
of turning "shouldn't"
into "is,"
ignoring the rules
of separateness.

ON LEARNING OF YOUR FATAL ILLNESS

Jealousy's tweezers
plucked our friendship
hair by hair,
until nothing was left
but smarting flesh.

Your digs drew blood
that hardened
into brick I used
to build a pyramid
of wrath
around my wounds,
an edifice invincible
to your remorse

but not to scuttlebutt
that soon, a pain
far greater than my own
would take your life—
news that chiseled
valentines into my walls,
reminding me

that in the changing climate
of the human heart,

forgiveness
is like summer rain,
waiting till the fields
are wasted,
then pouring in torrents
when it's too late.

ANOTHER FIGHT

The argument starts, as usual,
with an accusation intoxicated
on glass after glass of pettiness.

They sit together at the table,
the woman in her silk and lace,
the skinny youth in threadbare jeans,
each unable to stop the screams
that stagger toward the neighbors' stoops.

She threatens military school;
he thunders out the kitchen door,
flashing with obscenities
that make her eyeballs spin like cyclones.

Springing, wild-eyed, from her seat,
the woman reaches for the towel
that hangs above the scoured sink
and rips it into ragged strips,
as if to fashion bandages
for wounds inflicted on her soul,

while wide-eyed siblings
cower behind an easy chair,
long ago having decided to trade
the right to get angry for basic survival.

THE CURSE OF BEING FEMALE

You're long on looks,
my lover said
each time I stood
before the mirror,
scrutinizing my image
like a scribe
in search of errors
in a sacred scroll.

I rolled his words
in deafness
as I grimaced
at my random smears
and drooping serifs,
wishing I could
bury the parchment
and start again.

Decades later,
smudged with the ink
of middle age,
I page through photos
showing the self
I railed against

at seventeen
and twenty-one
and thirty-three,

wondering why
I cast aside
his accolades in days
that can no longer be,
yet still unable to perceive
unblemished strokes
still gracing me.

AFTER THE FUNERAL

A week ago, you were a stone in your spouse's shoe,
slowing her pace when she ached to race.

But now, you're the rock she leaned upon,
the diamond in her life's dark mine.

A week ago, you were a private,
hiding in a trench of ineptness.

But now, you are a general,
medaled for your every move.

A week ago, you were just a guy

who played with computers instead of his children
and came home from work with perfume on his suit.

But now, you're a Jesus, a Buddha, a Zeus,
enshrined by a crash for eternity.

FREQUENT FLYER

She creeps through the line
with her sometime dad,
who keeps dropping her hand
to wheel forward a rack
of suitcases crudely taped at the seams.

"Mama will meet you
when you land," the man repeats,
as a navy blue agent with silver wings
slips a boarding pass into the pouch
of her Snoopy pack.

"Enjoy your flight," the ticketer says,
mechanical as the conveyor belt
that snakes behind the counter top,
and she responds with the wilted smile
of a lily transplanted one time too many.

Kissing the father she'll visit
next Christmas or Fourth of July,
she heads alone to Gate 22 A,
where a flight attendant is saving a hug
embossed with her name.

I HOLD MY CAT

as the vet shaves fur
from a patch of paw
and inserts a needle
that glistens below
a plastic syringe
like the spire of a church
without religion.

The nurse's murmurs
of consolation
clash with my wails
like dissonant instruments
playing a dirge.

I could have avoided
this heart-cleaving scene
by saying good-bye
in the waiting room,

then handing the pet
who slept at my feet
for nineteen years
to a stethescoped Charon
who never saw her
bat at a string

or purr in the lap
of a smiling child.

But love is a drug
that numbs aversion,
transforming us
from foil to steel
in times of need,
if only for
a single moment.

HEARTBREAK

This feline stray
who claws the chairs and frays the rug
has sewn the hole you fell through
when our calico was laid beneath
the earth's green fur.

You giggle as he bats a string
and shriek as he chases
the mouse you made
from scraps of felt.

Hearing you purr
as you stroke his back,
I cannot bear to break the news
the vet delivered on the phone
about the bump we found last week—
a knuckle on the fist of Death.

Tonight we'll weep together
about all the shoulds that cannot be,
which feast on childhood's tender flesh
and build adulthood from the bones.

THE ILLUSION OF CONTROL

is the fuel of existence,
the petrol we daily
pump into our tanks,
pretending not to see it leak
into fleeting rainbows
on the pavement.

We belt our babies
into their seats,
command our teens
to be home by ten,
helmet our brains
on the bicycle path,
slather our skin
to screen out the sun,

while the radio
blares the latest
on the shooting
at the middle school,
the child whose transplant
didn't take,
the stabbing
at the brokerage firm,
the pilot who lowered
the flaps too soon.

How foolish
humans must appear—
but engines
cannot run on fear.

THE AWAKENING

When she was born, I swore
she'd never go to bed
with heartache's brine
upon her cheek.

I knitted her
a quilt of kisses
and tucked her into
a world without lumps,
laying her head
on an over-sized pillow
encased in possibility.

I shielded her
from the media's teeth,
removed the blades
from fairy tales,
plucked each weed
that tried to choke
the roses in her fertile soil,

until I caught her sobbing
over racial slurs
she'd heard at school,
and seven golden years of lies
turned to lead before my eyes.

ONE PARENT'S ANGUISH

*In memory of the murdered teens
at Columbine High School*

Blessed Jesus,

I kneel before you, away
from the cameras and microphones,
beseeching you to spare my son
from eternity in Satan's basement.

Despite what the police have said,
it was I, and not the boy,
who turned those students into ghosts
and wrote a dirge for security.

I should have asked
why he always wore black
and what he was doing day after day
with tools in the garage out back.

But I, the child of parents
who controlled me like a thermostat,
was only trying to give my son
the privacy I'd always craved.

I've lost him now to his own rage,
and guilt has moved in to take his place
with suitcases that bulge with groans
of a nation locked in throbbing grief.

If only I had known the past
can never be an able coach
in parenting, the game where rules
can change at any moment.

TOP PRIORITY

The woodpecker of chronic illness
drums its bill into my trunk,
extracting my will with its sticky tongue.

I long to gorge on pain pills,
to ignore the bells and flashing lights
that warn of an approaching train.

But as I kneel beside your bed,
sifting through the smiles and frowns
that shaped your day,

I realize that when I chose to give you life,
I chose to give away the right
to end my own.

FEAR

rises
to the ceiling
of being
like a helium balloon,
blowing
from room to room
as circumstance
opens and closes
the windows.

By day,
it bumps
against the walls
like a drunken bee;
by night,
it bobs
untethered
in the chop
of sleep.

We try to pop it
with words
of logic,
to stomp upon it
with denial.

Largo

But only
tenacious
fingers of faith
can untie
the knot
that gives it life.

HORMONES

They lurk in the trenches of femininity,
camouflaged in the regular rhythms
of heartbeat and breath,
waiting for the brain's command
to ravage my body's sleeping camp.

My sentinel listens for footsteps,
but the foe sneaks inaudibly
through the brush of bone and muscle,
suddenly springing, leaving
my infantry impotent
as a bayonet without a blade.

Waving a flag of subjugation,
I retreat to barracks
of medication and Chardonnay.

WAITING FOR THE PATHOLOGY REPORT

Apprehension
whorls through my day
like a hurricane,
flinging normalcy
this way and that
until it's reduced
to useless fragments.

I board up my house
with hopefulness,
then retreat
to the basement
with cans of distraction
and bottles of patience,
ignoring all warnings
to vacate before
the tempest lays waste
to my sanity.

If only escape
were as easy as taking
a train out of state,
or cellaring
like a yellow potato,
created with eyes
but lacking a heart
that can agonize.

MALIGNANT

I hear the word,

and compassion
begins to divide and spread,
taking over the seat
of my troubles
like a general
in a coup d'etat.

I envision you
in the chemo room,
tubed like a snorkeler
searching the murk
for rainbow reefs
where hope can feed.

I offer a meal, a book
to distract you
from pain and fatigue,
a ride for your children,
who still have lives
where a "D" on a test
or a loss for the team
is a reason to cry.

You politely decline,
explaining you don't
want to siphon my hours
like samples of blood,
and I can't make you see
that at times like this,
there's no worse imposition

than impotence.

IN THE HOSPITAL LOUNGE

the next of kin
blister in fluorescent sun,
trying to shove
the hours forward
like shuffleboard disks.
Sons and daughters,
husbands and wives
sip bad coffee
from paper cups
and chat about
the storm last night,
the latest rage
in video games,
the benefits
of instant rice—
anything
but the only thing
that dangles
in their psyches
like a spider idling
before the kill.

A man in sweats
escapes into snores;
the woman beside him
races through

her rosary beads.
Across the room,
a train of eyes
shuttles back and forth between
pages of print
and the open door,
where doctors in scrubs
periodically stop
to dole out news
like prescription drugs.

It's here that I hang,
a piñata of angst,
ready to burst
with a single swat
from the man in blue
who will call my name
when I least expect
and paint the future
in rainbow hues
or variegated
shades of gray.

AFTER CHEMO, YOU SHOW ME YOUR WIG

Once a radiant maple
in the grove of my beloved,
you've slowly shed your foliage
and coifed yourself in leaves of oak,
becoming your own fraternal twin,
similar and different as sugar and salt.

Uncertain what to say
about your strange, new way
of veiling winter barrenness,
I cap myself in quietude
and listen for the distant whispering
of sprigs.

PARTNER) IN DARKNE))

He meanders through
the cellar of eleven,
where the scents
of ripening adolescence
and fermenting childhood
enter each other
like May-December lovers.

I sit in the kitchen,
a floor above him,
wincing each time
I hear him bump
into bushels of comfort
he cannot see,
wishing he'd let me
turn on the light
a year or two
beyond his reach.

THE FALLING OUT

Your accusations rush like lemmings
down from fog-shrouded mountains

of grudges, trampling every speck of green
until they finally reach my sea.

Leaping gleefully into the swell,
they cannot swim, yet somehow manage

not to drown, as if they'd piled onto a raft
fashioned from their own black bile,

polluting undefiled blue
forever with their excrement.

THE SILENT TREATMENT

slinks through my soul
like a thief on the brink
of seizing my sanity's
hard-earned stash.

It feels its way through
the darkest chambers,
its fingers gloved
so as not to leave even
the faintest print.

Detecting the tiptoeing
of its feet, my heart-alarm
rings for the Reason Police,
who rush to the scene
in screaming cars.

But the culprit escapes
to a lair buried deep
in tenacity
and craftily schemes
for tomorrow's attempt.

THE LETTER

This newborn child
of violent silence
squalls in a sealed
blanket of paper,
about to be passed
into your hands.

Nourished on hurts
until it grew
too large to live
within the womb,
it thrashed its way through
a canal of decades,
emerging bloody
into today.

I wait for you
to feed it
or to leave it
on another's stoop,
where you won't be able
to hear its wails.

AFTER JOHN-JOHN'S PLANE CRASH

America's tears surge into the sea
that extinguished the fire of Hyannis Port,
he who once ignited the hearts
of a nation in grief with a single salute.

His name alights like a butterfly
on fluttering tongues in board rooms and bars,
sucking the nectar of sympathy
concocted for monarchs but not for moths.

Overcome by the scent of condolence,
the street people sprawl
at the country's feet, waiting
for someone to tell them the reason

compassion's attracted only to roses.

THE WEIGHT OF THOSE WHO CAME BEFORE

"You don't know what it feels like to be dogged by that giant."
— Johannes Brahms, 1874

Beethoven squatted
on Brahms's tract
of fertile land,
sowing rows
of intimidation,
until the Muse
could be induced
to serve a notice
of eviction,
making space
for a choke of notes
two decades old
to grow into a symphony.

If only art
would give us tools
to clear our fields
of those without
a deed or lease,
who over-plant
and over-reap
until our soil
can't yield a thing
except a solitary
scream.

NATURAL DISASTER

Ten-second tremblor.
Buildings buckle like colt knees.
Heaven turns to Hell.

Scores rot in rubble,
never again to ponder
the meaning of life.

Another hundred
are question marks, scrawled on Time
in the ink of angst.

But the far-off quake
barely makes it to page eight
of my newspaper.

GREETING MY GUEST
AFTER SEVERAL DECADES

Now that the globe on the bathroom light
has shed its shaggy jacket of dust

and the medicine cabinet that won't stay shut
has been scrubbed like the nails
of a child who recently played in the mud;

now that the stains
have been bleached from the sheets

and the floor where sneakers and backpacks have sparred
is as empty as a coliseum
a weekend after the final match;

now that I've managed to make my home
as perfect as the letter "o,"

perhaps you won't notice the blemishes
I've tried in vain to scour
from the porous grouting of my soul.

ON TURNING FORTY FIVE

The future
carols
outside
my
window.
I
hear
the
music,
but
not
the

words.

ANNUAL HAPPENING

When the yards
have canceled
their manicures
and the patio chairs
have migrated south
into paneled basements,

the snowmen line up
on suburban lawns,
sentinels guarding
winter's promise
of coziness.

Arrayed in woolen
scarves and hats,
with hand-knit mittens
dangling from their timber limbs,
they grin at passing
plows and blowers,

while on the other side
of town, children
trundle off to school
with fingers, necks,
and ears bedecked
in barrenness.

HE SAID, "WE'LL STILL BE FRIENDS"

Silver
was his love
for you,
dug with new tools
from the mine of youth
and shaped
into rings and bracelets
that you wore
with the pride
of a medalist.

You polished
and buffed
to preserve its luster,
but couldn't prevent
the alchemist
of circumstance
from changing it
to stainless steel—

a half-breed
less prized
than sterling's child,
but better able
to weather the nicks
and gouges of time.

AMERICAN GOTHIC II

A canoe of a man,
battered by storms
that have rotted his hull
and peeled his paint,
flails his paddles
in pools of trash
that stagnate in cans
on a downtown street.

Fishing a large paper cup
from the muck,
he greedily drinks,
grateful that somebody's
thirst was slaked
before the vessel
was fully drained.

I watch him imbibe
from my automobile
as I drive home from lunch
at a trendy cafe,
while the radio lists
the ten hottest gifts
under five hundred dollars
for Christmas this year.

FLOUNDERING

Your weather whirls
from May to November
and back again,
a madcap dervish mesmerized
by chanting only you can hear.

I robe you in magnolia
when your leaves turn the color
of funeral dirges
and drop into caskets that days ago
were beds for tulips and daffodils.

It's then I discover that tufts of satin
can't insulate a naked branch.

Helpless as a baby robin
hatched before the spring arrives,
I peck and peck at your frozen field,
hoping to find a tidbit or two
on which we both can feed.

BLOCKED

Poetry melts into winter slush,
never to return, or so it seems.

My paper pleads for crocuses,
gets only mud and frozen leaves.

Puddles distort perspective
like a Picasso portrait

as I forage for buds, finding
only November's corpses.

I gather dried fertility
and place it in a vase of hope,

leaving space between the stalks
for sprigs of green.

WAITING ROOM

My child fidgets under a portrait
the dentist's wife painted to match the carpet,
her tennis shoes thwacking the leg of her seat
like canvas woodpeckers, her gaze flapping
between my face and a white-coated woman
calling out names.

Picking up a magazine,
I read about victims of Saddam Hussein,
teenagers shot at an Arkansas school,
a woman whose baby was cut from her womb
by a barren couple steeped in despair.

I try to feel blessed, to embrace
these sad cousins once removed,
but all I can do is curse the fall
that shattered my daughter's first big tooth,
making no news, but meaning much more
than the more important.

TO LAST NIGHT'S DREAM

You lumber into midnight
like a grizzly bear in search of prey
and paw at my serenity.

I toss you tidbits from my day,
hoping I can satisfy your appetite
with the mundane,

but it is soul food that you crave.

Your teeth draw blood
that stains the spotless dark with angst
and wakes my spouse as drop by drop,

it seeps into his snores.
He shakes my shoulder, calls my name,
until you bolt into the woods

and I begin to count the hours
till dawn transforms you into
a timorous, gray mouse.

Largo

VARIATIONS ON A THEME

I

My neon libido
barges into
your beige desire
in quest of a yes.

I clamp my fingers
over its mouth,
hoping to silence
its shrill entreaties
before they shatter
the fragile glass
of our attachment.

But passion bites back,
drawing blood
that will stain our love
until you bind
the wound with strips
of mutuality.

II

I long to feed
the creature gamboling
in your groin,

but obligation
has raided my pantry,
devouring lust
with shoulds and musts.

I restock after work,
while I'm cooking
or looking after the kids,
but my shelves are still bare
at the end of the day,
when you ransack
my cupboard
for savory bits.

If only you'd walk
through the brambly fields
of womanhood,
you'd bleed the red
of realization
instead of the black
of deprivation.

WHAT IFS

consume the spirit
nibble by nibble,
savoring the subtle
flavor of sane-ness
we labor for decades
to cultivate.

Tucking their napkins
under their chins,
they salivate
like Pavlov's dog
each time the phone
rings late at night
or when the dreaded
letter comes.

Then quietly,
they feast upon
the tenderest tidbits
of existence,
leaving not a single crumb
for the jealous tongue
of serenity.

DIFFERENT STYLES

You, a child
of the pastel East,
indulge my need
to fill
the stillness
with chatter thick
as a traffic jam,
and ask yourself
if I, a child
of the neon West,
will come to know
that in the masterpiece
of life,
the rests
give meaning
to the notes,
the negative space
to the brush's strokes.

VIVACE

RAVINIA PARK:
A HAIKU SYMPHONY OF SUMMER

I

An expanse of grass
turns into an orchestra
of picnic baskets

II

A fanfare engraves
the clabbered air of July
with a brass chisel

III

Citronella scent
intoxicates the fireflies
as the crowd quaffs sound

IV

Airplanes harmonize
with crickets and cicadas
while the stars tango

V

Couples on blankets
perform flashy cadenzas
without conductors

VI
Darting through the dark,
children are sixty-fourth notes
on the staff of night

VII
A commuter train
and honking station wagons
play a sad coda

WILD ANIMAL PARK, SAN DIEGO

Skyscraper of fauna
saunters toward
the jeep where biscuits
beckon from extended hands
that wave like the savanna grass.

She thrusts a muzzle
mottled with expectancy
between the squeals and camera snaps,
reaching out a slimy tongue
that runs the length of Africa.

Gaping at her fluid flanks,
her liquid eyes
where heedfulness
plays tag with trust, her neck
bedecked in scarves of grace,

I'm mute as she, stupefied
by Nature's creativity
in shaping water, earth, and air
into this matchless masterpiece
we call giraffe.

JAZZ

To spell it is to know it:

j,
dotted like the notes
in a syncopated bar,
imitating on the tongue
the stroke of a brush
on a cymbal or drum;

a,
a morsel of melancholy
passed from Dixie to Detroit
and over the ocean
on platters of steel,
wood, and brass;

z,
repeated like a boogie bass,
buzzing with the freedom
of a bee that flies
wherever its instincts
tell it to go.

Rarely played
on the stage of the brain,

it resonates
in a smoky room
at the back of the soul,

where inhibition cannot go.

SURVIVOR

The speaker sits on the lighted stage,
a virtuoso of pain and loss
performing horror while incredulity
dances in the listeners' veins.

With nouns and verbs, she plays
a black cacophony of capture,
of lives transformed to empty staffs,
of transposition into ash.

Then gradually, she modulates
from minor into major key,
concluding with a coda of hope
only an angel could compose.

Astounding that this crone who knows
the strokes of evil's steel baton
can hear the future symphonize
without a note of dissonance.

A GLIMPSE OF THE FUTURE

She sizzles on a concrete griddle,
kneeling by the green bean seeds
she planted in a pot last week.

The one o'clock sunshine
tongues her curls like a zealous lioness
cleaning her cubs, playfully pawing

the beads of sweat on her freckled nose,
the scab on her knee, the mosquito bites
she capriciously named Annette and Marie.

She pats the soil, fills her plastic
watering can, and ever so gently,
slakes the thirst of the tender shoots,

crooning to them as I did to her
those hot afternoons
when she herself was newly hewn.

At only six, it's easy to see
the loving mother
she someday will be.

WINTER METAPHOR

One week after the second biggest
blizzard on record, the railroad embankment
becomes a Dalmatian, its white flanks splotched
with slush from passing cars and trucks.

Stroking its coat with snow-weary eyes,
I suddenly notice a make-shift shrine
planted capriciously on a drift
like a toddler's kiss.

Its plastic tulips and daffodils
put clown paint on the day's grim face;
its pink balloons bob on commuters' amazement,
inviting all to come and play.

I run for my train and marvel
at the way each tiny reminder of spring
enables us to endure the recurring
flurries and squalls that winter brings.

EXHIBITION

This space that last week
was a prairie of carpet
with ladders and scaffolds
scattered like weeds

has mutated into
a block of Manhattan,
dazzling as a skyline at noon.

I stroll through the booths,
where genius disguised
in wood and ceramic, metal and glass,
smiles as it poses for porous eyes.

There are no spires or hymnals here,
no holy inscriptions
or windows depicting Biblical tales,

yet, as I peruse
the creations of human
minds and hands, I hear
the exalted singing of angels.

FOR MY SIXTY-SOMETHING FRIEND

You sail through aging
blithely as a bride's bouquet,
strewing blooms
for tomorrow to hold
between its teeth
as it habaneras
in sequined shoes.

Inhaling your fragrance,
I reach up to catch
a lily or rose
to veil the odor
of mid-life malaise,
managing only
to grope the air
like a baby too young
to grab what she's after.

Placing a bowl
on a table veneered
in peeling patience,
I wait for the wind
to pluck me a few
of your redolent petals.

ON RETURNING TO THE PIANO

Long ago, my fingers
thrummed the piano keys
like drops of rain, washing
debris from the air of my being.

The strings and my avidity
teamed to make the hours flee
to Camelots of rhythm
and Edens of tonality.

Now, once again,
the ivory smile beckons me,
though middle age has kidnapped
my dexterity and memory.

I wriggle on the padded bench,
shaking out my kinks like sheets,
and straighten up my frowning spine.
Uncertain as a first-date kiss,

I start to play, and music
staggers through the room,
a reveler who doesn't know
he's had a bit too much to drink.

My hands arpeggio through pain,
and muscles languish as I reach

for chords as tall and brawny
as athletes on a football field

while joy crescendos through my soul,
drowning out the body moans
and sour notes, and once again,
I feel whole, if only momentarily.

OUR FIRST FIGHT

Goose-stepping into my confidence,
your anger smashes
the tinted glass
that shielded me
from the glare of the past.

Clicking the heels
of its pointed boots,
it salutes your needs
and scrawls swastikas
on what cannot be.

A chamber of death
beckons with fingers
invisible to all but me.
I enter and inhale deeply,
praying for a hasty end,

amazed when forgiveness
rounds the bend
in a brand new jeep
to unlock the door
and command my release.

THE DINERS

frolic beside America's two-lane highways,
plucking trucks and minivans with greasy
fingers, dropping them into lonely lots
stained with rainbows of motor oil,

each a clone, sporting identical
cakes and pies and Jello squares
that rotate near the hostess stand
like planets covered in plastic wrap,

salad bars, with macaroni
lost in dunes of mayonnaise
and bits of fruit and marshmallow
that flail in waves of whipping cream,

waitresses coifed in cotton candy,
their makeup thick as August air,
spilling Sanka on burgundy uniforms,
calling every customer "hon,"

balloon-gut truckers
and blue-haired women in polyester
who salt their stew without tasting it
and call impatiently for their checks.

Driving by, you'll hear the diners
scoff at the china and tiramisu
of the Plaza and Ritz,
knowing it is they and theirs

who make our nation what it is.

A FIRST AND LAST ATTEMPT AT QI GONG*

The crone on the video
flaunts her vitality
like a diamond,
jumping and jogging
to show the verve
she garnered after surgery
with just an hour
of daily practice.

A white-robed master
appears on the screen
and gently dispatches
my Westerness eastward,
instructing my hands
to waft over my head
like bony balloons.

I scoop up a life-force
that thumbs its nose
at the thinking mind
and ladle it over
my head and shoulders,
trying to wash away
layers of pain,

until Rationality
lassos my body
with belly-laughs
and pulls me back
to the world of my birth,
where healing is packaged
in tamper-proof plastic.

*Qi (pronounced "chee") is the Chinese term for energy. Qi gong is an ancient healing method using slow, fluid movements to manipulate qi throughout the body. Today, millions of people still practice qi gong worldwide.

HONESTY

child shaper
child snatcher

spouse keeper
spouse beater

friend net
friend knot

colleague treat
colleague threat

the snows of truth
glisten and nip

don't go out
without a muffler

FIRST PROM

1971

Sprayed and shellacked,
I pose for the camera, my smile
stiff as my gown of chiffon.

My manicured hands clasp a beaded bag
jam-packed with makeup
for hourly touch-ups.

Feeling at one
with my orchid corsage,
whose splendor masks its fragility,

I offer my arm to a rented tux
and totter on my three-inch heels
into the awe of adulthood.

1998

My daughter grins at the viewfinder,
defying the wind to whisk away
the roses planted in her hair.

She's easy as a baby's breathing,
sheathed in satin that flows like lava
over her curves.

I snap the photo, wondering if Kodak
can capture her jaunty confidence
to frame and hang,

a reminder that sometimes,
the apple succeeds
in falling far away from the tree.

SUMMER'S HERALD

Cottonwood seeds
reel to the golden
fiddle of June,
do-si-do'ing
until they're too dizzy
to see where they're going.
Heeding the calls
of a yodeling wind,
they swing their partners
and promenade
across the fields
on weightless feet,
gauzing screens,
freeing sneezes,
making tow-heads
of brunettes.

If only I could
lilt through life
like cottonwood,
twirling to desire's patter,
never caring
where I landed.

THE BOYS OF THE BLUE LINE

Subway babies,
piccolos in pants
that puddle at the ankle,

pulling commuters
from newspapers
with magnets of tenacity.

Cola-colored swaggerers,
dissipating August heat
with prepubescent cool,

rapping in a baffling language,
blowing notes on crumpled straws,
whistling into folded fingers,

while one too young
to keep the beat
solicits coins in a toy tambourine.

Next week, they'll sit
in rows of desks
and listen to their teachers drone,

but today, they're kings
of the underground,
with power to be heard and seen.

ON HEARING A KLEZMER BAND

You *hora* from the ear to the heart
to the deepest hollows of the bones,
where your scarlet sonorities
mix into marrow, oxygenating
the blood of my heritage.

You make me think of *kreplach*
and blintzes, of brides and grooms
raised high on chairs by smiling men
in loose, black suits, of *shtetl* women
trading gossip on synagogue steps.

Ah, Klezmer, lively child
of Joy and Suffering,
long banished from your land of birth
by Führer fury louder
than your clarinets and violins—

how wonderful to hear you
here across the sea, unbridled
as your spirit and your quirky style,
stirring up my Jewishness
far more than prayer or ritual.

HOW IT HAPPENS

A poem slumbers under
the soil of the humdrum,
hidden from view like a tulip bulb.

Sensing its presence,
I ravage the earth like a ravenous squirrel,
finding only stone and clay.

I gorge on seeds of busyness
that feed my mind but leave my heart
as barren as a winter field

until, forgotten, the poem explodes
through the ground, full-grown,
guffawing at my astonishment.

BEWILDERMENT

"What happens to all the wedding gowns
when the music stops and the guests go home?"

"Cupid changes the tulle and lace
into snowflakes that bewitch the eye
like a baby's smile."

"What happens to all the baby teeth
after the Tooth Fairy carries them off?"

"Buffed with the cloth of eternity,
they hang in Wyoming's midnight sky
like ornaments on a Christmas tree."

"What happens to all the Christmas trees
after we put them out on the street?"

"The needles become the prickly words
that leap from the lips of the winter-weary,
who know that spring's still months away."

"What happens to all the nettled phrases
when blizzards stop and spring arrives?"

"Some are recycled, and some
are dispatched to the city dump
to linger forever like Styrofoam cups."

"What happens to all the Styrofoam cups
when there's no more room to pile them up?"

"They change into questions
that no one has ever been able to answer,
though many have tried."

"What happens to all the unanswered questions
the centuries pass from one to the next?"

"They turn into children,
who bother and baffle,
until they grow up and forget how to ask."

TRANSFORMATION

When the ash of November
dissolves into the pearl of December;

when pages of dots
mutate into a stagger of sound;

when the diamond crawls out
of the lapidary's rock;

when lines entwine into cartoon people,
doodling smiles on humdrum lives;

when cocoa bean bitterness
transfigures into chocolate bliss;

when the gawk of a girl
ripens into an Aphrodite—

Transformation kisses Existence,
blessing it with divinity.

A YEAR IN THE MIDWEST

January
Squalling newborn
We swaddle our goose bumps in soup and tea.

February
Sneeze of the calendar
Candy hearts mate with analgesics.

March
Winter's caboose
The end of the line is finally in sight.

April
Tear duct of angels
Umbrellas contort like circus performers.

May
Country milkmaid
The landscape guzzles pails of pastel.

June
Midas's finger
The sun flaunts fourteen-carat bracelets.

July
Middle child
Schedules scream for Leisure's attention.

August
Rubato in summer's sonata
Languor conducts cicada choruses.

September
Houdini of the seasons
Beach bags transform into backpacks.

October
Crayola's daughter
Red and yellow tango to harvest syncopation.

November
Corroded bone
Nature yawns, revealing missing teeth.

December
Frenzied anthill
The year scurries out as the picnic ends.